Gratitude

"Perhaps nothing helps us make the movement from our little selves to a larger world than remembering God in gratitude. Such a perspective puts God in view in all of life, not just in the moments we set aside for worship or spiritual disciplines. Not just in the moments when life seems easy." __Henri Nouwen

Gratitude

Gene Allen Groner

To:

____

From:

____

I will give thanks to you, Lord, with all my heart;

I will tell of all your wonderful deeds.

—Psalm 9:1

To God

Dear Heavenly Father,

Please accept my humble gratitude

For all the blessings of life.

You have blessed me abundantly

And I can never repay you, I know.

But I can dedicate my life to your service

And I gladly do so.

Thank You, God.

In the precious name of Jesus Christ,

Amen.

Gratitude

Gene Allen Groner

Introduction

When I was a child, my mother taught me a simple song that has remained with me all my life. It goes like this:

"When I'm worried and I can't sleep,

I count my blessings instead of sheep,

And I fall asleep counting my blessings."

I wish I could tell you why I decided to write this book about gratitude, but I just don't know, other than to say that somehow the seed was planted in my mind this morning as I was editing a book I had written.

I suppose it came to me the same way all my other books have come to me—God planted a seed in my mind and heart to gratefully testify of his eternal love.

Perhaps I should share with you the story of how I began writing in the first place. I will do that in Chapter Two.

I am reserving the first chapter for Jesus Christ. He is number one in my book.

Chapter One

For the Gift of Jesus Christ

Warner Sallman's Head of Christ, pictured on the previous page, is the picture of Jesus I saw every Sunday morning and evening at church.

My mother always took my brother and I to church on Sunday morning. In addition, I liked to go on Sunday evening and Wednesday evening. Each time I would see the face of Jesus hanging in a frame on the wall behind the lectern. The image gave me comfort. It helped ground me for the week ahead.

I always knew Jesus would be there at the church, waiting for me. Today, Jesus is still with me, watching and waiting for me to call on him whenever I need strength or comfort. I count on him for guidance in my daily life and in my writing. He is always faithful and dependable in every need I may have. He is trustworthy, and he is my constant companion. He brings me inner peace and joy.

True joy is the lot of the Christian. As such, it is to be a part of the Christian experience wherever we go. To radiate joy and a joyful countenance is the hallmark of the Christian life, and is a sign that the individual has aligned himself or herself with the person of Jesus Christ.

Jesus said, "I am come that they might have life, and that they might have it more abundantly."—John 10:10 KJV

When I traveled to Israel in 2008 during the week of Passover, I felt the presence of Jesus Christ on several occasions. On one of them, I had the privilege of worshiping in the Garden of Gethsemane, where Jesus had prayed after the Passover meal (the Last Supper) with his disciples.

Just a short distance east of the old city of Jerusalem, I walked up the Mount of Olives to the Garden of Gethsemane. It was a warm sunny day in April, a bird was softly singing in the garden, and I sat down on a small stone bench under an olive tree to meditate and pray.

The pathways around me were all lined with beautiful spring flowers, and the garden was quiet and peaceful. It seemed that I was the only one in the garden when I bowed my head in prayer. I thanked my heavenly Father for such a wonderful opportunity as this. Here I was in the Garden of Gethsemane, where Jesus kneeled to pray to the Father, asking for "this cup to be taken from me—nevertheless, thy will not mine be done."

As I began to pray I felt humble to be in the same garden where Jesus knelt to pray, and to walk in his footsteps and pray to the Father in Heaven in that sacred place. I could feel his presence with me and the warmth of the Holy

Spirit while I thanked him for his love and the unspeakable gift of his life.

Then I remembered the circumstances of Jesus' betrayal and arrest, and the terrible suffering he endured—suffering and death on a rough Roman cross so that the gift of salvation might come to me, and to all those who believe and accept Jesus as Lord and Savior. All these thoughts came into my mind as I continued to pray, giving thanks for God's gift of grace and mercy, and for the ultimate sacrifice of Christ. It was such a humbling experience, and I still think of it often, especially in my quiet moments of prayer and meditation.

In the garden there is an ancient Olive Tree that some say was living at the time of Jesus, but our guide Rose said it is only 1500 years old (*only* 1500 years). I can't begin to explain the feeling I had while walking in the garden. It is inexplicable and powerful, standing there and looking across the Kidron Valley at the Golden Gate of the eastern Temple Wall, the gate through which Christ will enter upon his return.

I walked along a garden pathway lined with flowers and bushes, and I sat down on a small stone bench to pray. As I looked eastward toward the Temple Mount, I heard a songbird in a nearby Olive tree singing ever so softly.

After a few minutes of prayer, thanking God for his amazing grace and the blessing of being present in the garden where Jesus walked and prayed, I could feel the warmth of his Spirit flowing over me, reminding me of his continuing presence. I was overcome with joy and gratitude. The peace of Christ was with me.

Chapter Two

For the Gift of Writing

Let me tell you my personal testimony of how and why I began writing.

Not long ago, I was in a Christian bookstore in Independence, Missouri. Looking through the displays, I noticed a new book written by Mark Batterson titled, Draw the Circle. The title was catchy, so I picked it up and looked through the pages, until I fell upon a particular page where the author issued a challenge. I'm always up to new challenges, so I read on.

The challenge read as follows: Pray on your knees at the same time every day for 40 days and watch for the miracles that come to you. Wow! I thought. I have prayed all my life, but not on my knees, so I thought I might give it a try and see what happens. I was in one of those down cycles that Christians get in to from time to time, and I needed a boost—a spark in my heart that could ignite a flame of passion for life once again—a direction and a purpose.

That night as I was preparing for bed, I remembered the book and the challenge. So I took off my shoes—Moses was told to do this in the Book of Exodus out of respect for God—and I knelt beside my bed to pray. I said, "Dear Lord, I am accepting this challenge and I ask for your perfect will to be done in my life. May I once again feel the flame of passion in my life. I am willing to do whatever you want me to do. In Jesus' name, amen."

For the next 40 days I prayed this same prayer, in the same way, and at the same time. On the morning of the 41st day, I awoke early with the thought in my mind to write a book. I had never written a book before, so this would be a new experience for me. Believing was the Lord who planted that idea in my mind, I went to my computer and opened up Microsoft Word to begin. As I did so, the words started to flow from my mind onto the pages, and I haven't stopped writing since that day. Day after day, word after word, I write one Christian book, blog, or magazine article after another. The Lord has given me a fresh new lease on life, and a passion for learning and writing that I love.

It is now 2020 and I have written and published more than 40 Christian books, in addition to quite a number of magazine articles on faith and spirituality. I am amazed at how the Holy Spirit continues to bring me ideas and empowers me to write, sharing my testimony of the peace and love of Our Lord and Savior Jesus Christ. Thanks be to God.

It all began with a simple prayer. The reason I write is to witness of the love and peace of Jesus Christ and his kingdom here on earth.

All the honor and glory goes to God, the Father of us all, and I am more than happy to give him all the credit—he deserves it all. I am reminded of the Christian song by William and Gloria Gaither titled, "Jesus is Lord of All."

"Lord of all, Lord of all, Jesus is Lord of all. All my possessions and all my life, Jesus is Lord of all."

The greatest desire of my heart is for the testimony of Jesus' love and peace to go to every person and every nation on earth, doing my part to help fulfill the Great Commission,

"Therefore go and make disciples of all nations, baptizing them in the name of the Father and of the Son and of the Holy Spirit, and teaching them to obey everything I have commanded you. And surely I am with you always, to the very end of the age." (Matthew 28:19-20 NIV)

I am grateful for the gift of writing. After reading one of my books of poetry, my wife told me I have a gift for writing poetry.

I have written many books of poetry, including The Garden of Eden, Prayers and Poems of Christ, Summer: a Season of Hope, 2020 Poems, and The Nature of Angels. A number of other books I have written contain some of my poetry as well.

My brother Wayne is perhaps my greatest helper, making suggestions to improve my writing (he is an accomplished writer and historian). He told me not long ago that I have a God-given gift of writing. Thank you, Wayne. Anything that I am able to do well I consider to be a gift from my Creator, for which I am very thankful.

I am grateful for their kind comments and suggestions—they are most helpful to me and I take them to heart.

My books are published by Amazon/Kindle in both paperback and eBook—the eBook format presents the pictures and images in full color. All of my books are available from my author website and the Kindle Store. Here is the link:

https://www.amazon.com/Gene-Allen-Groner/e/B077YTVSJZ

Email address geneallengroner@gmail.com

I thoroughly enjoy writing, and I write every day. It is something that not only gives me enjoyment, it gives me an outlet for my creative energies.

I am not a gifted artist, but occasionally I do like to draw or paint, particularly scenes from nature. My eldest daughter is a gifted artist, but she keeps very busy with her full-time career and raising two of my beautiful grandchildren. I love all of my five children and nine grandchildren, and they are all talented in their own ways.

Chapter Three

For the Gift of Home and Family

I am very grateful for the gift of home and family. Mother Teresa said it best: "A life not lived for others is not a life."

I love Mother Teresa, and I have read a number of her books and books written about her. As a matter of fact, one of the books I wrote a while back is titled, Saint Teresa of Calcutta. It was a true pleasure and an honor to write about such a wonderful and inspiring person, completely devoted to the family of God.

Mother Teresa gave her life to Christ in 1910 at the age of 18, and spent most of her many years of ministry as a nun, serving the "poorest of the poor" in Calcutta, India. She founded the worldwide Missionary Sisters of Charity in 1950, which manages homes for people dying of HIV/AIDS, leprosy and tuberculosis, in addition to the many other outreach and community ministries of the sisters such as soup kitchens, dispensaries and mobile clinics, children's- and family-counseling programs, orphanages, and schools.

Saint Teresa had a lot to say about the home and family. Here is one of her many stories:

"Don't forget that there are many children, many children, many men and women who haven't got what you have. And remember to love them until it hurts. Sometime ago, this to you will sound very strange, but I brought a child from the street, and I could see in the face of the child that the child was hungry. God knows how many days that she had not eaten. So I gave her a piece of bread. And then the little one started eating the bread crumb by crumb. And I said to the child, eat the bread, eat the bread.

And she looked at me and said: I am afraid to eat the bread because I'm afraid when it is finished I will be hungry again. This is a reality, and yet there is a greatness of the poor.

One evening a gentleman came to our house and said, there is a Hindu family and the eight children have not eaten for a long time. Do something for them. And I took rice and I went immediately, and there was this mother, those little one's faces, shining eyes from sheer hunger. She took the rice from my hand, she divided it into two and she went out. When she came back, I asked her, where did you go? What did you do? And one answer she gave me: They are hungry also.

She knew that the next door neighbor, a Muslim family, was hungry.

What surprised me most, not that she gave the rice, but what surprised me most, that in her suffering, in her hunger, she knew that somebody else was hungry, and she had the courage to share, share the love.

And this is what I mean, I want you to love the poor, and never turn your back to the poor, for in turning your back to the poor, you are turning it to Christ. For he had made himself the hungry one, the naked one, the homeless one, so that you and I have an opportunity to love him, because where is God? How can we love God?

It is not enough to say to my God I love you, but my God, I love you here. I can enjoy this, but I give up. I could eat that sugar, but I gave that sugar.

If I stay here the whole day and the whole night, you would be surprised by the beautiful things that people do, to share the joy of giving.

And so, my prayer for you is that truth will bring prayer in our homes, and from the foot of prayer will be that we believe that in the poor it is Christ. And we will really believe, we will begin to love. And we will love naturally, we will try to do something.

First in our own home, next door neighbor in the country we live, in the whole world.

And let us all join in that one prayer, God give us courage to protect the unborn child, for the child is the greatest gift of God to a family, to a nation and to the whole world.

God bless you!" _Mother Teresa

Even as I am writing this about Mother Teresa, I can sense the Lord guiding and blessing my words. Without God's help and inspiration there would be no writing from me—this I know for certain. Thank You, God.

"Bring prayer in our homes," Teresa said.

"Bring prayer in our homes, and from the foot of prayer will be that we believe that in the poor it is Christ. And we will really believe, we will begin to love. And we will love naturally, we will try to do something. First in our own home, next door neighbor in the country where we live, in the whole world."

My home and family are the cement that holds me together—makes me whole. Without them I would be like a ship without a rudder, wandering aimlessly across the sea of life. Without my home and family there would be no stability in my life.

My home and family are much more than a place and a group of people. They are love itself. They are a blessing that is so great it is beyond description, other than to say they are what gives meaning to my life.

I need my home and family, and they need me. God made us that way, and we wouldn't want it any other way.

Each night before I go to bed, I get down on my knees and thank God for the blessings of the day, for my home and family. I pray that the peace of Christ will dwell in our hearts and in our home. Then I pray for the homeless and the refugees in the world—and there are millions of them, unfortunately. Finally I pray for all the animals, and for the environment that we have been systematically destroying—the beautiful world that God created for our benefit.

We all need to pray for the love of our families every day, just as Mother Teresa has said:

"If you want to bring happiness to the whole world, go home and love your family."

"Whatever you do for your family, your children, your husband, your wife, you do for God. All we do, our prayers, our work, our suffering, is for Jesus."

"It is easy to love the people far away. It is not always easy to love those close to us. Bring love into your home, for this is where our love for each other must start."

Bernardino Luini - Holy Family with the

Infant Son John

Mother Teresa believed so strongly in the power of prayer that, if families chose to pray with each other regularly, they would become authentic witnesses of peace.

"Love begins at home, and it is not how much we do…but how much love we put in that action." –Mother Teresa

"The child is the beauty of God present in the world, that greatest gift to a family."

Guido Reni - Saint Joseph and the Christ Child

Our world is in need of healing. The community, the nation, the world, all need the healing blessing of Jesus Christ. Where do we begin, you ask. We must begin at home. We must learn to love each other in our families. Only there can we begin to heal the world. Only there can we begin to heal ourselves. The family and the home. Start with prayer. Live with love.

Mother Teresa said, "The way you help heal the world is that you start with your own family."

Bernardino Luini - The Virgin Holding the Sleeping Child

As I write this, I realize that I do not always show the love to my family that they need and deserve. I have been guilty of speaking harshly at times, and even saying things I shouldn't.

But I can do better. We all can do better. Let us pray for forgiveness, remembering the prayer that Jesus taught his disciples, The Lord's Prayer, also called the Our Father:

"Our Father who art in heaven,

Hallowed be thy name.

Thy Kingdom come, thy will be done

On earth as it is in Heaven.

Forgive us our trespasses

As we forgive those who trespass against us,

And lead us not into temptation

But deliver us from evil,

For thine is the Kingdom, and the Power,

And the Glory forever. Amen"

Chapter Four

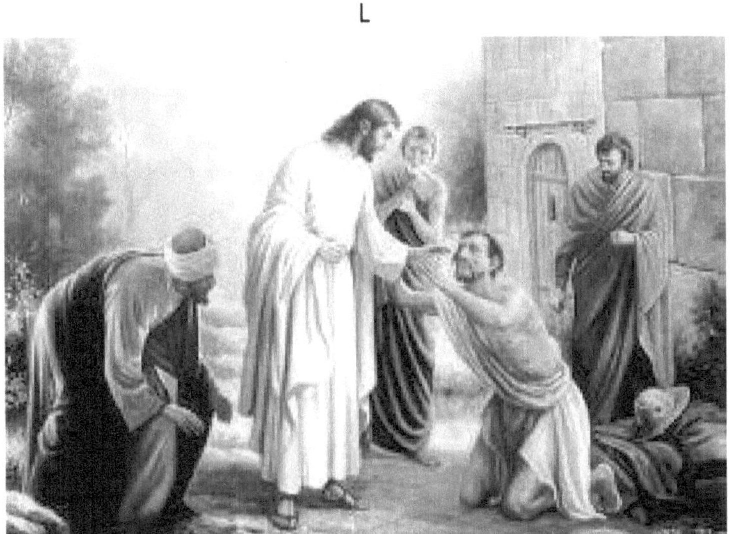

For the Gift of Life and Health

I just finished watching DreamWorks movie Shrek 2, the 2004 sequel to the movie Shrek.

The reason I mention it here is because it speaks to one of the world's most serious problems—differences in the appearance and behavior of people in our communities, nations, and all over the world.

God created all kinds of people—people of different sizes, shapes, colors, and languages. And what did God say when he created the people and the world we live in?

He said, "It is very good!"

"Then God looked over all he had made, and he saw that it was very good!"—Genesis 1:31 NLT

Have you ever heard it said, "God doesn't make junk?" Of course you have; we all have.

If God doesn't make junk, and he said that everything and everyone he made is very good, then why do we argue and fight against those who are different from us? Good question!

The story of Shrek and Fiona and her family in Shrek 2 tells of their trip to Far, Far Away Kingdom where her parents live—the king and queen. As the story unfolds, Shrek and Fiona drink a magic potion that changes them from homely, green Ogres into a beautiful couple like her parents and all the people in their Kingdom. Everyone looks alike. Get the picture? No differences in their appearance or behavior or the way they talk.

Everyone is happy, right?

Wrong!

Fiona decides she loves Shrek and wants them to be just as they were before—homely Ogres.

The poster on the previous page shows the Ogres Shrek and Fiona and their friends from the swamp where they live.

What is significant about the movie is this:

Love and happiness have nothing to do with appearance or culture or where you live. To God, everybody and everything he created is beautiful—very good!

Sometimes I think our world is upside down.

So many people and institutions place value on other people based on appearance, culture, the way they talk or walk or any of a dozen other things—that is opposite of how God made us.

We are made to love God and love each other. Only then can we see the real beauty in other people and in nature. Only then will we know real joy and happiness the way God intended:

Jesus said it in John 10:10,

"I am come that they might have life, and that they might have it more abundantly."

"As for me and my house, we will serve the Lord."

Be happy! Love one another. Start at home.

Chapter Five

For the Beauty of the Earth

In 2007 the movie Evan Almighty made its debut, starring Steve Carell and Morgan Freeman, and featured one of my favorite actors John Goodman.

I watched the film in 2020 on TNT, and really liked it.

The story is about a newly elected congressman, Evan Baxter and his encounter with God (Morgan Freeman). God tells Evan to build an ark, and the story unfolds as a re-telling of the biblical account of Noah's Ark.

One line from the movie really struck me. God told Evan, "You want to know how to change the world, son—one act of random kindness at a time."

The line is in the movie because Congressman Baxter ran on the campaign promise to "change the world." Obviously the show is a comedy, but beneath the humor (and there is plenty of it) there is a real life message. It is summed up in the words of God, "...change the world...one act of random kindness at a time."

When God created the world, with all the animals and plants and people, he said that if was very good. I want a world that is like the one God created—clean, beautiful, good. Help me make it that way again, as it once was. My book titled Pride and Pollution, deals with making the earth beautiful again. Let's all help.

"Change the world, one random act of kindness at a time."

God, played by Morgan Freeman, told Evan's wife that "life is about love, two by two, just like the animals on Noah's Ark."

This movie is full of important messages of faith, love, and kindness—the most important things that I need to practice more of in my life. Let me ask you this question:

What is most important in your life?

From the Director of Bruce Almighty
STEVE CARELL   MORGAN FREEMAN
Evan ALMIGHTY
A Comedy Of Biblical Proportions

Chapter Six

For Angels

Let me begin this final chapter the same way I began the book.

I'd like to tell you a personal story.

I Believe in Angels

"For he shall give his angels charge over thee, to keep thee in all thy ways."

__Psalm 91:11 KJV

Ever since I was eight years old and in the third grade, I have believed in angels.

Riding my bicycle home from the grocery store one Saturday morning, I was struck by a car and knocked into the ditch. The car didn't stop to check on me. A little ruffled but otherwise unharmed, I brushed myself off and rode safely home. Mother met me at the door and could easily see my dirty shirt. Showing no surprise she asked, "Are you alright?" When I told her what had happened and she could see that I was okay she said, "I knew you would be safe because I prayed to God that he would send his angels to protect you." From that moment on I knew that angels were real, even if I couldn't see them.

More recently, in 2017 I was involved in a car wreck and woke up in a hospital. I barely remember the accident but will never forget how I was saved by an angel. The accident occurred in the country. For miles around there was no one but me. I hit a guard rail and totaled the car. I later learned that a young woman named Rachel found me and took me to the hospital. I never saw her, never heard her voice. But I knew without a doubt that God had sent an angel to rescue me.

God has always revealed himself through the ministry of angels. In chapter six of the Book of Daniel, God sent an angel to close the jaws of the lions after Daniel was thrown into the lions' den. And we all know about the angel Gabriel's announcement to Mary,

"The Holy Ghost shall come upon thee, and the power of the Highest shall overshadow thee: therefore that holy thing which shall be born of thee shall be called the Son of God" (Luke 1:35).

In her book, The Hiding Place, Corrie ten Boom tells of her remarkable experience in the Nazi concentration camp at Ravensbruck. Upon arrival, she and her sister Betsie, along with all the other women prisoners were told to remove all their clothes and put them in a pile. They were then handed their prison dress. Guards then searched the women before taking them to their barracks. Corrie had a Bible hidden in her clothing, along with some woolen underwear for her sister. Those items made a bulge in her dress and could easily be detected by the guards who searched the women again before taking them to their barracks. Before the final search, Corrie ten Boom prayed, "Lord, cause now thine angels to surround me, and let them not be transparent today, for the guards must not see me." The woman in front of her had hidden a woolen vest under her dress. It was taken from her. They let Corrie pass, for they did not see her. Betsie right behind her was searched.

Don't ever think that your angels have left you. They are always there. Sometimes they are busy working behind the scenes to bring you happier times, so never, ever give up!

Miracles happen today like they did in the Old Testament and the New Testament times. Angels continue to minister in our lives today, as they have throughout all of history. They watch over us and protect us, and they guide us always toward our Father in Heaven. We may not see or hear them, but they are real and they are all around us.

I believe in angels.

The Bible reminds us to "Be not forgetful to entertain strangers: for thereby some have entertained angels unawares" (Hebrews 13:2).

The Holy Bible is full of accounts of angelic ministry. Here are just a few of them:

Angels guided Moses as he led the Israelites from bondage by the Pharaoh.

In the Book of Exodus, we read the story of how an angel of the Lord was leading Moses and his people daily through the wilderness and into the Promised Land.

"The Egyptians will know that I am the LORD when I am honored through Pharaoh, his chariots, and his horsemen." Then the Angel of God, who had gone before the camp of Israel, withdrew and went behind them. The pillar of cloud also moved from before them and stood behind them, so that it came between the camps of Egypt and Israel. The cloud was there in the darkness, but it lit up the night. So all night long neither camp went near the other. Then Moses stretched out his hand over the sea, and all that night the LORD drove back the sea with a strong east wind that turned it into dry land. So the waters were divided, and the Israelites went through the sea on dry ground, with walls of water on their right and on their left. Then the Egyptians chased after them— all Pharaoh's horses, chariots, and horsemen— and followed them into the sea. At morning watch, however, the LORD looked down on the army of the Egyptians from the pillar of fire and cloud, and He threw their camp into confusion."__Exodus 14:18-26 Berean Study Bible

The story of Daniel in the Lions' Den

We all know the story of Daniel and the Lions' Den—I learned it in my Sunday school class, and it was one of my favorite stories. It is found in the Book of Daniel, chapter six:

It pleased Darius to appoint 120 satraps to rule throughout the kingdom, with three administrators over them, one of whom was Daniel. The satraps were made accountable to them so that the king might not suffer loss.

He distinguished himself among the administrators and the satraps by his exceptional qualities that the king planned to set him over the whole kingdom. At this, the administrators and the satraps tried to find grounds for charges against Daniel in his conduct of government affairs, but they were unable to do so. They could find no corruption in him, because he was trustworthy and neither corrupt nor negligent. Finally these men said, "We will never find any basis for charges against this man Daniel unless it has something to do with the law of his God."

So these administrators and satraps went as a group to the king and said: "May King Darius live forever! The royal administrators, prefects, satraps, advisers and governors have all agreed that the king should issue an edict and enforce the decree that anyone who prays to any god or human being during the next thirty days, except to you, Your Majesty, shall be thrown into the lions' den. Now, Your Majesty, issue the decree and put it in writing so that it cannot be altered—in accordance with the law of the Medes and Persians, which cannot be repeated." So King Darius put the decree in writing.

Now when Daniel learned that the decree had been published, he went home to his upstairs room where the windows opened toward Jerusalem. Three times a day he got down on his knees and prayed, giving thanks to his God, just as he had done before. Then these men went as a group and found Daniel praying and asking God for help. So they went to the king and spoke to him about his royal decree: "Did you not publish a decree that during the next thirty days anyone who prays to any god or human being except to you, Your Majesty, would be thrown into the lions' den?"

The king answered, "The decree stands—in accordance with the law of the Medes and Persians, which cannot be repealed."

Then they said to the king, "Daniel, who is one of the exiles from Judah, pays no attention to you, Your Majesty, or to the decree you put in writing. He still prays three times a day." When the king heard this, he was greatly distressed; he was determined to rescue Daniel and made every effort until sundown to save him.

Then the men went as a group to King Darius and said to him, "Remember, Your Majesty, that according to the law of the Medes and Persians no decree or edict that the king issues can be changed."

So the king gave the order, and they brought Daniel and threw him into the lions' den. The

king said to Daniel, "May your God, whom you serve continually, rescue you!"

A stone was brought and placed over the mouth of the den, and the king sealed it with his own signet ring and with the rings of his nobles, so that Daniel's situation might not be changed. Then the king returned to his palace and spent the night without eating and without any entertainment being brought to him. And he could not sleep.

At the first light of dawn, the king got up and hurried to the lions' den. When he came near the den, he called to Daniel in an anguished voice, "Daniel, servant of the living God, has your God, whom you serve continually, been able to rescue you from the lions?"

Daniel answered, "May the king live forever! My God sent his angel, and he shut the mouths of the lions. They have not hurt me, because I was found innocent in his sight. Nor have I ever done any wrong before you, Your Majesty."

The king was overjoyed and gave orders to lift Daniel out of the den. And when Daniel was lifted from the den, no wound was found on him, because he had trusted in his God.

At the king's command, the men who had falsely accused Daniel were brought in and thrown into the lions' den, along with their wives and children. And before they reached the floor of the den, the lions overpowered them and crushed all their bones.

Then King Darius wrote to all the nations and peoples of every language in all the earth:

"May you prosper greatly!

"I issue a decree that in every part of my kingdom people must fear and reverence the God of Daniel.

"For he is the living God

   and he endures forever;

his kingdom will not be destroyed,

   his dominion will never end.

He rescues and he saves;

   he performs signs and wonders

   in the heavens and on the earth.

He has rescued Daniel

   from the power of the lions."

So Daniel prospered during the reign of Darius and the reign of Cyrus the Persian.

When Mary, the mother of Jesus, was only a young girl of 14 to 16 years of age, the angel Gabriel appeared to her.

Here is that well-known beginning to the Christmas story from the Gospel of Luke:

Luke 1:26-38 New Life Version (NLV)

Gabriel Speaks to Mary

Six months after Elizabeth knew she was to become a mother, Gabriel was sent from God to Nazareth. Nazareth was a town in the country of Galilee. He went to a woman who had never had a man. Her name was Mary. She was promised in marriage to a man named Joseph. Joseph was of the family of David. The angel came to her and said, "You are honored very much. You are a favored woman. The Lord is with you. *You are chosen from among many women."

When she saw the angel, she was troubled at his words. She thought about what had been said. The angel said to her, "Mary, do not be afraid. You have found favor with God. See! You are to become a mother and have a Son. You are to give Him the name Jesus. He will be great. He will be called the Son of the Most High. The Lord God will give Him the place where His early father David sat. He will be

King over the family of Jacob forever and His nation will have no end."

Mary said to the angel, "How will this happen? I have never had a man." The angel said to her, "The Holy Spirit will come on you. The power of the Most High will cover you. The holy Child you give birth to will be called the Son of God.

"See, your cousin Elizabeth, as old as she is, is going to give birth to a child. She was not able to have children before, but now she is in her sixth month. For God can do all things." Then Mary said, "I am willing to be used of the Lord. Let it happen to me as you have said." Then the angel went away from her.

Annunciation (c. 1472–1475), Uffizi, is thought to be Leonardo da Vinci's earliest complete work.

It has been a great pleasure to create this book for you. I sincerely hope you have enjoyed reading it and will want to share it with a friend—or better yet, purchase several copies to give away as part of your efforts to share the love of Christ with others.

Visit my author page at https://www.amazon.com/stores/Gene-Allen-Groner/author/B077YTVSJZ

Email me at geneallengroner@gmail.com

Thank you sincerely. May God bless you.

Gene

And now I would like to close with this prayer:

Our Father in Heaven,

Thank you for the gift of Christ and the Holy
Spirit, and for all the many gifts and blessings
we receive from your gracious bounty. I am so
grateful that you sent your son Jesus to live
among us, and to show us the way of love.
Thank you for his life, his forgiveness, and for
his sacrifice on the cross for our salvation. I
pray that everyone will come to receive Jesus
Christ as the Lord and Savior of their life, and
in so doing inherit the Kingdom of Heaven
prepared by you. May our faith and love
increase day by day, and may we continue to
grow in our faithfulness and our witness of
Jesus Christ. In the precious name of Jesus,
our Savior and friend, amen.

Be Kind to Everyone

"I AM WITH
YOU ALWAYS,
UNTIL THE END
OF THE AGE."
©LPi

About the Author

Gene Allen Groner is a Christian writer and author of more than 40 inspirational books and numerous magazine articles. He lives in Independence, Missouri with his wife of 55 years, a retired public health nurse. His interests include reading and writing, gardening, and volunteer work in the community. He is listed in Who's Who in Missouri, and is a lifetime member of the National Honor Society in Psychology, Psi Chi. Gene has a Master of Arts in Religion degree with honors from Park University in Parkville, MO. He also attended the University of Hawaii and St. Paul School of Theology. He and his family are lifetime members of the Colonial Hills congregation in Blue Springs, MO.

https://www.amazon.com/Gene-Allen-Groner/e/B077YTVSJZ

geneallengroner@gmail.com

Books by Gene Allen Groner in paperback and Kindle eBook available on his author website at https://www.amazon.com/Gene-Allen-Groner/e/B077YTVSJZ

Journey of a Disciple

The Garden of Eden

Native American Prayers Poems and Legends

Native American Horses

Native American Fine Art

Fine Art Paintings

Micah's Fine Art

Fine Art of Sassan Filshoof

Son of the Most High

These Three Remain

The Helper: a Discourse on the Holy Spirit

Hallowed Be Thy Name

Deborah: Prophetess and Warrior

Saint Teresa of Calcutta

From Shepherd to King: the Story of David

The Nature of Angels

A Book of Prayers

Speak To This People: Prophets and Prophecies

For Such a Time as This: the Story of Esther

Prayers and Poems of Christ

In the Beginning

Take Off Your Sandals: the Story of Moses

Silver-Tongued Prophet: the Story of Isaiah

My God is Yahweh: the Story of Elijah

Meditations (in English and Portuguese)

Evangelist Billy Graham

World's Greatest Missionary: the Apostle Paul

2020 Poems

Stairway to Heaven

Full of Grace

Jesus' Hands Are Kind Hands

The Kingdom of Heaven

Women in the Bible

Testify

Revelation

The Cross

The Road to Emmaus

Pentecost

Jesus Loves You